MW01078059

Fractions, Decimals, & Percents
Math Workbook

(Includes Repeating Decimals)

Improve Your Math Fluency Series

Chris McMullen, Ph.D.

Fractions, Decimals, & Percents Math Workbook (Includes Repeating Decimals)

Improve Your Math Fluency Series

Copyright © 2012 Chris McMullen, Ph.D.

All rights reserved. This includes the right to reproduce any portion of this book in any form. However, teachers who purchase one copy of this book, or borrow one physical copy from a library, may make and distribute photocopies of selected pages for instructional purposes for their own classes only. Also, parents who purchase one copy of this book, or borrow one physical copy from a library, may make and distribute photocopies of selected pages for use by their own children only.

CreateSpace

Science / Mathematics / Fractions
Education / Specific Skills / Mathematics / Fractions

ISBN: 1477524886

EAN-13: 978-1477524886

Contents

Making the Most of this Workbook

- Mathematics is a language. You can't hold a decent conversation in any language if you have a limited vocabulary or if you are not fluent. In order to become successful in mathematics, you need to practice until you have mastered the fundamentals and developed fluency in the subject. This *Fractions, Decimals, & Percents Math Workbook* will help you improve the fluency with which you convert between fractions, decimals, and percents.

- This workbook is conveniently divided into 5 chapters so that you can focus on one basic skill at a time. In chapter 1, practice converting fractions into decimals and percents. In chapter 2, practice converting decimals into fractions and percents. In chapter 3, practice converting percents into fractions and decimals. Chapters 4 and 5 involve converting between fractions and repeating decimals.

- The introduction has concise instructions describing how to perform each type of conversion. These instructions are followed by a few examples. Use these examples as a guide until you become fluent in the technique.

- After you complete a page, check your answers with the answer key in the back of the book. Practice makes permanent, but not necessarily perfect: If you practice making mistakes, you will learn your mistakes. Check your answers and learn from your mistakes such that you practice solving the problems correctly. This way your practice will make perfect.

- Math can be fun. Make a game of your practice by recording your times and trying to improve on your times, and recording your scores and trying to improve on your scores. Doing this will help you see how much you are improving, and this sign of improvement can give you the confidence to succeed in math, which can help you learn to enjoy this subject more.

How to Solve the Problems

Multiplying Decimals

To multiply numbers with decimals, stack them vertically. Unlike adding and subtracting numbers with decimals, align the **factors** (the two numbers that you are multiplying together) by their rightmost digits (not by the decimal point). Don't worry if the decimal places don't match – as long as the rightmost digits are aligned. Then multiply the numbers the same way that you would multiply whole numbers. Align the intermediate numbers by the rightmost digit the same way that you would ordinarily align them if you were multiplying whole numbers together. Lastly, you need to determine where to put the decimal point in the **product** (that's the final answer). Count the number of digits in each factor that are to the right of their decimal points. Add these two numbers together. Place the decimal point of the product such that the number of digits to the right of its decimal point equals the sum of the numbers of digits to the right of the factors' decimal points. You may need to add leading zeroes to make this possible.

EXAMPLES

$$4.23 \times 0.078 =$$

$$\begin{array}{r} {\scriptstyle 1\ 2} \\[-2pt] {\scriptstyle 1\ 2} \\[-2pt] 4.23 \\ \times\ 0.078 \\ \hline 0.03384 \\ 0.29610 \\ \hline 0.32994 \end{array}$$

$$0.002 \times 0.5 =$$

$$\begin{array}{r} 0.002 \\ \times\ 0.5 \\ \hline 0.0010 \end{array}$$

In the first example, the factor 4.23 has 2 digits to the right of its decimal point and the factor 0.078 has 3 digits to the right of its decimal point. Therefore, the product, 0.32994, has 5 digits to the right of its decimal point. That's how you determine where to put the decimal point in the answer. In the second example, the 0.002 has 3 digits to the right of its decimal point and 0.5 has 1 digit to the right of its decimal point. The answer, 0.0010, must then have 4 digits to the right of its decimal point. Notice that two leading zeroes had to be added (after the decimal point) in order to achieve this. Trailing zeroes of numbers with decimal points may be removed. For example, the answer 0.0010 may also be expressed as 0.001.

Converting Fractions to Decimals

To divide numbers with decimals, arrange them in long division form just as you would if you were dividing whole numbers. Then divide the numbers the same way that you would divide whole numbers. However, instead of writing a remainder, add trailing zeroes to the **dividend** (that's the number you are dividing into) as needed. The decimal position of the **quotient** (the final answer) comes about quite naturally. That is, as you carry out the long division, you multiply digits of the **quotient** (the answer above the dividend) with the **divisor** (that's the number you are dividing by, which appears at the left). You'll have to put the decimal position in the right place (using the rule for multiplying numbers with decimals) in the quotient to make this work.

For example, in 3/4, the dividend is 4, the divisor is 3, and the quotient is 3/4 or 0.75. The fraction 3/4 can be written as long division in the form $4\overline{)3.00}$ (see below).

Study the examples below and refer to them as needed to guide your practice – until you can solve the problems by yourself. When you complete a page of exercises, check your answers in the back of the book – and learn from any mistakes that you might have made.

EXAMPLES

$$5/8 = 5 \div 8 \qquad 1/16 = 1 \div 16$$

$$3/4 = 3 \div 4 \qquad 12/5 = 12 \div 5$$

$4\overline{)3.00}$	$5\overline{)12.0}$	$8\overline{)5.000}$	$16\overline{)1.0000}$
0.75	2.4	0.625	0.0625
2.80	10.0	4.800	0.9600
0.20	2.0	0.200	0.0400
0.20	2.0	.160	0.0320
0	0	0.040	0.0080
		0.040	0.0080
		0	0

Notice that 3 divided by 4 and 12 divided by 5, for example, would normally be expressed with remainders as 0R1 and 2R2, but by adding the trailing zeros to 3 and 12 to turn them into 3.00 and 12.0, the answers could be expressed as decimals rather than with remainders. In fact, all remainder problems of whole number long division can be expressed in decimal form. For example, 25 divided by 4, which would normally be 6 with a remainder of 1, is found to be 6.25 using the method of long division with decimals. Try it!

Converting Fractions to Repeating Decimals

Sometimes, the method of long division with numbers with decimals never ends! That is, you need to keep adding trailing zeroes to the dividend forever. Fortunately, when this happens the digits repeat in a pattern. This is called a **repeating decimal**. For example, 1 divided by 3 results in 0.3333... Try it and see for yourself. The digit 3 repeats forever. This repeating decimal is denoted by adding a bar over it: $0.\overline{3}$. The $\overline{3}$ represents an infinite sequence of 3's. So $0.\overline{3}$ is actually larger than 0.3. Similarly, 11 divided by 9 equals $1.\overline{2}$. Try it yourself.

You might get a repeating sequence of digits rather than a single repeating digit. For example, 20 divided by 11 equals $1.\overline{81}$. Try it and see. In this case, the 81 sequence repeats over and over. That is, $1.\overline{81}$ represents 1.818181... The 81 repeats forever. The sequence may be long. For example, 3 divided by 7 equals $0.\overline{428571}$.

Study the examples below (and there is another on the back cover) and refer to them as needed to guide your practice – until you can solve the problems by yourself. When you complete a page of exercises, check your answers in the back of the book – and learn from any mistakes that you might have made.

EXAMPLES

5/6 = ?	6/11 = ?	7/18 = ?	25/22 = ?

```
   0.833          0.5454          0.388            1.13636
6 )5.000       11 )6.00000     18 )7.0000       22 )25.0000
   4.8             5.5             5.4              22
   0.20            0.50            1.60             3.0
   0.18            0.44            1.44             2.2
   0.020           0.060           0.160            0.80
                   0.055           0.144            0.66
5/6 = 0.83̄         0.0050          0.0160           0.140
                   0.0044                           0.132
                   0.00060      7/18 = 0.38̄         0.0080
                                                    0.0066
                6/11 = 0.54̄̄                         0.00140
```

$$25/11 = 1.1\overline{36}$$

Notice that the 20 repeats at the end of the first example, and that the 50 and 60 repeat, alternately, in the second example. This is how you know if and when the decimal is repeating.

Converting Nonrepeating Decimals to Fractions

A nonrepeating decimal can be converted to a fraction as follows: (1) Figure out what power of ten you need to multiply the decimal by in order to remove the decimal point. Here are some examples: Multiply 0.4 by 10 to make 4, multiply 0.12 by 100 to make 12, and multiply 0.375 by 1000 to make 375. (2) Use the number without a decimal point as the numerator and use the power of 10 from Step 1 as the denominator. For the examples above, you would get 4/10, 12/100, and 375/1000. (3) If the resulting fraction is reducible, cancel the greatest common factor to reduce it. For the examples above, 4/10 becomes 2/5 by dividing numerator and denominator by 2, 12/100 becomes 3/25 by canceling the greatest common factor of 4, and 375/1000 becomes 3/8 by dividing through by 125.

EXAMPLES

$$0.25 = 25/100 = 1/4 \quad , \quad 1.5 = 15/10 = 3/2 \quad , \quad 0.004 = 4/1000 = 1/250$$

Converting Repeating Decimals to Fractions

A repeating decimal can be converted to a fraction as follows: (1) Multiply by the power of 10 needed so that the repeating digits will disappear if the original repeating decimal is subtracted from the new number. As examples, multiply $0.\overline{3}$ by 10 to make $3.\overline{3}$, multiply $0.4\overline{1}$ by 10 to make $4.\overline{1}$, and multiply $.\overline{030}$ by 1000 to make $30.\overline{030}$. When you multiply by the power of 10, remember that the overbar represents a sequence of digits that repeats forever. (2) Subtract the original repeating decimal from the new one (that you obtained in Step 1 by multiplying by a power of 10). This subtraction cancels the repeating decimal. Use this as the numerator. Subtract 1 from the power of 10 and use that as the denominator. In the above examples, you would get 3/9, 3.7/9, and 30/999. (3) If the numerator is a decimal, multiply both the numerator and denominator by the power of 10 needed to make the numerator an integer. (4) If the resulting fraction is reducible, cancel the greatest common factor to reduce it. For the examples above, 3/9 becomes 1/3, 37/90 is irreducible, and 30/999 becomes 10/333.

EXAMPLES

$$0.\overline{6} = (6.\overline{6} - 0.\overline{6})/9 = 6/9 = 2/3 \quad , \quad 0.\overline{45} = (45.\overline{45} - 0.\overline{45})/99 = 45/99 = 5/11$$

$$1.\overline{7} = (17.\overline{7} - 1.\overline{7})/9 = 16/9 \quad , \quad 0.\overline{148} = (148.\overline{148} - 0.\overline{148})/999 = 148/999 = 4/27$$

$$4.\overline{3} = (43.\overline{3} - 4.\overline{3})/9 = 39/9 = 13/3 \quad , \quad 1.4\overline{7} = (14.\overline{7} - 1.4\overline{7})/9 = 13.3/9 = 133/90$$

$$0.0\overline{58} = (5.8\overline{58} - 0.0\overline{58})/99 = 5.8/99 = 58/990 = 29/495$$

Relating Percents to Decimals (and Fractions) and Decimals to Percents

To convert a decimal to a percent, simply multiply by 100 and add a % sign to the end of the number. To convert a percent to a decimal, do just the opposite: That is, divide by 100 and remove the % sign.

EXAMPLES

$$0.42 = 0.42 \times 100\% = 42\% \quad , \quad 1.3 = 1.3 \times 100\% = 130\% \quad , \quad 0.1 = 0.1 \times 100\% = 10\%$$
$$75\% = 75/100 = 0.75 \quad , \quad 250\% = 250/100 = 2.5 \quad , \quad 0.8\% = 0.8/100 = 0.008$$

To convert a percent to a fraction, first convert the percent to a decimal and then convert the decimal to a fraction. Similarly, to convert a fraction to a percent, first change it to decimal form and then make the percentage.

Chapter 1: Converting Fractions to Decimals and Percents

Instructions: First, convert each fraction to a decimal following the technique described on page 6. Next, convert the decimal to a percent according to the instructions on page 9.

(1) 1/2

(2) 7/10

(3) 2/5

(4) 5/4

(5) 3/8

(6) 4/25

(7) 1/16

(8) 7/20

(9) 1/5

(10) 9/4

(11) 5/2

(12) 7/50

Instructions: First, convert each fraction to a decimal following the technique described on page 6. Next, convert the decimal to a percent according to the instructions on page 9.

(1) 1/400

(2) 19/5

(3) 19/8

(4) 23/40

(5) 6/25

(6) 29/50

(7) 39/40

(8) 27/10

(9) 17/100

(10) 21/100

(11) 8/25

(12) 14/5

Instructions: First, convert each fraction to a decimal following the technique described on page 6. Next, convert the decimal to a percent according to the instructions on page 9.

(1) 21/20   (2) 7/2   (3) 13/80   (4) 17/10

(5) 17/16   (6) 25/8   (7) 33/10   (8) 17/80

(9) 37/20   (10) 15/4   (11) 21/100   (12) 2/25

Instructions: First, convert each fraction to a decimal following the technique described on page 6. Next, convert the decimal to a percent according to the instructions on page 9.

(1) 17/4   (2) 24/5   (3) 11/100   (4) 1/16

(5) 29/80   (6) 3/400   (7) 11/4   (8) 29/20

(9) 13/16   (10) 23/2   (11) 27/50   (12) 25/16

Instructions: First, convert each fraction to a decimal following the technique described on page 6. Next, convert the decimal to a percent according to the instructions on page 9.

(1) 1/40   (2) 17/100   (3) 19/16   (4) 9/400

(5) 13/16   (6) 17/20   (7) 17/8   (8) 9/200

(9) 23/100   (10) 39/400   (11) 3/8   (12) 19/50

Instructions: First, convert each fraction to a decimal following the technique described on page 6. Next, convert the decimal to a percent according to the instructions on page 9.

(1) 3/4

(2) 12/25

(3) 27/5

(4) 27/100

(5) 11/100

(6) 5/4

(7) 23/25

(8) 11/8

(9) 19/2

(10) 17/16

(11) 17/80

(12) 31/20

Instructions: First, convert each fraction to a decimal following the technique described on page 6. Next, convert the decimal to a percent according to the instructions on page 9.

(1) 19/40   (2) 21/10   (3) 1/200   (4) 17/40

(5) 7/10   (6) 27/50   (7) 27/50   (8) 1/16

(9) 21/5   (10) 23/25   (11) 4/5   (12) 12/25

Instructions: First, convert each fraction to a decimal following the technique described on page 6. Next, convert the decimal to a percent according to the instructions on page 9.

(1) 31/200

(2) 1/50

(3) 37/50

(4) 7/25

(5) 17/20

(6) 23/4

(7) 23/200

(8) 9/16

(9) 15/4

(10) 17/5

(11) 7/40

(12) 39/20

Instructions: First, convert each fraction to a decimal following the technique described on page 6. Next, convert the decimal to a percent according to the instructions on page 9.

(1) 17/2   (2) 17/40   (3) 31/50   (4) 31/100

(5) 18/25   (6) 21/10   (7) 23/8   (8) 17/4

(9) 11/8   (10) 23/4   (11) 31/10   (12) 7/100

18

Instructions: First, convert each fraction to a decimal following the technique described on page 6. Next, convert the decimal to a percent according to the instructions on page 9.

(1) 21/10

(2) 31/400

(3) 17/400

(4) 7/20

(5) 9/16

(6) 23/10

(7) 13/2

(8) 31/10

(9) 3/8

(10) 12/5

(11) 9/4

(12) 21/50

Instructions: First, convert each fraction to a decimal following the technique described on page 6. Next, convert the decimal to a percent according to the instructions on page 9.

(1) 1/8　　　　　(2) 29/25　　　　　(3) 9/16　　　　　(4) 21/2

(5) 3/4　　　　　(6) 31/100　　　　　(7) 9/200　　　　　(8) 9/40

(9) 17/40　　　　　(10) 39/50　　　　　(11) 28/5　　　　　(12) 11/10

Instructions: First, convert each fraction to a decimal following the technique described on page 6. Next, convert the decimal to a percent according to the instructions on page 9.

(1) 17/100

(2) 7/10

(3) 28/25

(4) 1/16

(5) 31/40

(6) 9/400

(7) 9/8

(8) 22/25

(9) 13/400

(10) 25/8

(11) 23/16

(12) 8/25

Instructions: First, convert each fraction to a decimal following the technique described on page 6. Next, convert the decimal to a percent according to the instructions on page 9.

(1) 13/80   (2) 7/200   (3) 17/4   (4) 13/40

(5) 3/25   (6) 2/25   (7) 21/400   (8) 17/8

(9) 37/50   (10) 11/20   (11) 21/4   (12) 31/80

Instructions: First, convert each fraction to a decimal following the technique described on page 6. Next, convert the decimal to a percent according to the instructions on page 9.

(1) 37/80   (2) 25/4   (3) 11/400   (4) 9/16

(5) 7/40   (6) 33/40   (7) 17/16   (8) 9/80

(9) 27/25   (10) 2/25   (11) 39/50   (12) 1/5

Instructions: First, convert each fraction to a decimal following the technique described on page 6. Next, convert the decimal to a percent according to the instructions on page 9.

(1) 39/200   (2) 21/200   (3) 23/4   (4) 13/50

(5) 4/25   (6) 11/50   (7) 7/8   (8) 29/400

(9) 27/40   (10) 9/10   (11) 29/5   (12) 31/40

Instructions: First, convert each fraction to a decimal following the technique described on page 6. Next, convert the decimal to a percent according to the instructions on page 9.

(1) 3/16   (2) 1/4   (3) 3/100   (4) 31/20

(5) 1/50   (6) 18/25   (7) 13/400   (8) 13/16

(9) 5/4   (10) 1/16   (11) 17/8   (12) 1/10

Instructions: First, convert each fraction to a decimal following the technique described on page 6. Next, convert the decimal to a percent according to the instructions on page 9.

(1) 21/16

(2) 4/25

(3) 21/400

(4) 13/10

(5) 13/8

(6) 11/4

(7) 6/25

(8) 21/50

(9) 28/25

(10) 31/400

(11) 13/2

(12) 17/10

Instructions: First, convert each fraction to a decimal following the technique described on page 6. Next, convert the decimal to a percent according to the instructions on page 9.

(1) 27/20   (2) 23/200   (3) 9/5   (4) 27/200

(5) 29/400   (6) 7/16   (7) 19/8   (8) 31/10

(9) 5/4   (10) 39/40   (11) 23/8   (12) 19/200

Instructions: First, convert each fraction to a decimal following the technique described on page 6. Next, convert the decimal to a percent according to the instructions on page 9.

(1) 37/80   (2) 21/8   (3) 25/16   (4) 11/200

(5) 13/80   (6) 15/16   (7) 28/5   (8) 23/8

(9) 3/50   (10) 13/50   (11) 29/50   (12) 19/16

Instructions: First, convert each fraction to a decimal following the technique described on page 6. Next, convert the decimal to a percent according to the instructions on page 9.

(1) 1/2

(2) 9/40

(3) 5/4

(4) 3/10

(5) 9/25

(6) 25/16

(7) 7/50

(8) 31/50

(9) 29/100

(10) 19/80

(11) 37/20

(12) 31/100

Chapter 2: Converting Decimals to Fractions and Percents

Instructions: First, convert each decimal to a fraction following the technique described on page 8. Next, convert the decimal to a percent according to the instructions on page 9.

(1) 0.75

(2) 0.1

(3) 2.5

(4) 0.3

(5) 3.2

(6) 0.375

(7) 1.25

(8) 0.8

(9) 0.5

(10) 0.01

(11) 0.05

(12) 0.95

Instructions: First, convert each decimal to a fraction following the technique described on page 8. Next, convert the decimal to a percent according to the instructions on page 9.

(1) 0.4375   (2) 3.75   (3) 0.0425   (4) 1.5

(5) 1.5625   (6) 0.0825   (7) 0.84   (8) 0.78

(9) 0.0475   (10) 0.05   (11) 0.2   (12) 1.12

Instructions: First, convert each decimal to a fraction following the technique described on page 8. Next, convert the decimal to a percent according to the instructions on page 9.

(1) 6.25   (2) 0.045   (3) 2.9   (4) 3.5

(5) 2.9   (6) 0.6875   (7) 3.5   (8) 0.26

(9) 0.625   (10) 0.225   (11) 9.5   (12) 0.3

Instructions: First, convert each decimal to a fraction following the technique described on page 8. Next, convert the decimal to a percent according to the instructions on page 9.

(1) 2.625

(2) 0.0475

(3) 0.25

(4) 0.45

(5) 0.16

(6) 0.0325

(7) 0.7

(8) 2.5

(9) 0.14

(10) 0.25

(11) 1.125

(12) 1.625

Instructions: First, convert each decimal to a fraction following the technique described on page 8. Next, convert the decimal to a percent according to the instructions on page 9.

(1) 0.29   (2) 2.3   (3) 0.0675   (4) 0.0525

(5) 0.0625   (6) 0.3375   (7) 0.2875   (8) 0.4125

(9) 0.64   (10) 6.5   (11) 1.25   (12) 3.75

Instructions: First, convert each decimal to a fraction following the technique described on page 8. Next, convert the decimal to a percent according to the instructions on page 9.

(1) 0.07   (2) 7.5   (3) 0.005   (4) 3.4

(5) 0.42   (6) 3.5   (7) 0.07   (8) 1.9

(9) 0.275   (10) 1.35   (11) 0.42   (12) 0.02

Instructions: First, convert each decimal to a fraction following the technique described on page 8. Next, convert the decimal to a percent according to the instructions on page 9.

(1) 0.48   (2) 0.4375   (3) 0.07   (4) 0.85

(5) 1.05   (6) 0.175   (7) 1.25   (8) 1.45

(9) 0.03   (10) 2.1   (11) 0.23   (12) 0.58

Instructions: First, convert each decimal to a fraction following the technique described on page 8. Next, convert the decimal to a percent according to the instructions on page 9.

(1) 0.065   (2) 2.6   (3) 3.6   (4) 1.3125

(5) 0.0975   (6) 0.11   (7) 9.5   (8) 2.75

(9) 1.1875   (10) 7.5   (11) 1.625   (12) 0.0825

Instructions: First, convert each decimal to a fraction following the technique described on page 8. Next, convert the decimal to a percent according to the instructions on page 9.

(1) 1.375   (2) 0.0025   (3) 0.34   (4) 0.4375

(5) 0.8   (6) 0.02   (7) 1.875   (8) 0.08

(9) 11.5   (10) 0.225   (11) 2.9   (12) 2.5

Instructions: First, convert each decimal to a fraction following the technique described on page 8. Next, convert the decimal to a percent according to the instructions on page 9.

(1) 0.825　　　　　(2) 6.5　　　　　(3) 0.15　　　　　(4) 4.5

(5) 2.875　　　　　(6) 0.4　　　　　(7) 10.5　　　　　(8) 0.88

(9) 0.66　　　　　(10) 2.375　　　　　(11) 0.825　　　　　(12) 3.3

Instructions: First, convert each decimal to a fraction following the technique described on page 8. Next, convert the decimal to a percent according to the instructions on page 9.

(1) 0.325   (2) 0.46   (3) 1.1   (4) 1.85

(5) 1.0625   (6) 2.625   (7) 2.375   (8) 0.52

(9) 0.35   (10) 0.525   (11) 0.975   (12) 5.25

Instructions: First, convert each decimal to a fraction following the technique described on page 8. Next, convert the decimal to a percent according to the instructions on page 9.

(1) 0.015   (2) 0.125   (3) 3.125   (4) 2.5

(5) 0.0875   (6) 0.34   (7) 1.5625   (8) 0.0175

(9) 2.125   (10) 3.25   (11) 0.275   (12) 0.33

Instructions: First, convert each decimal to a fraction following the technique described on page 8. Next, convert the decimal to a percent according to the instructions on page 9.

(1) 0.125 (2) 0.58 (3) 0.45 (4) 0.475

(5) 0.19 (6) 1.25 (7) 2.75 (8) 1.4

(9) 0.475 (10) 0.275 (11) 3.125 (12) 0.01

Instructions: First, convert each decimal to a fraction following the technique described on page 8. Next, convert the decimal to a percent according to the instructions on page 9.

(1) 0.26   (2) 0.46   (3) 0.975   (4) 1.4375

(5) 0.24   (6) 3.125   (7) 0.425   (8) 1.125

(9) 2.25   (10) 0.975   (11) 0.96   (12) 0.0625

Instructions: First, convert each decimal to a fraction following the technique described on page 8. Next, convert the decimal to a percent according to the instructions on page 9.

(1) 0.66

(2) 3.125

(3) 2.625

(4) 0.6875

(5) 3.125

(6) 0.85

(7) 0.68

(8) 1.8

(9) 0.0675

(10) 2.1

(11) 1.1875

(12) 0.0075

Instructions: First, convert each decimal to a fraction following the technique described on page 8. Next, convert the decimal to a percent according to the instructions on page 9.

(1) 2.875

(2) 0.12

(3) 1.4

(4) 4.5

(5) 0.28

(6) 0.15

(7) 0.0875

(8) 4.25

(9) 1.4375

(10) 9.5

(11) 0.08

(12) 0.525

Instructions: First, convert each decimal to a fraction following the technique described on page 8. Next, convert the decimal to a percent according to the instructions on page 9.

(1) 6.25   (2) 1.4375   (3) 2.7   (4) 1.375

(5) 1.85   (6) 1.8   (7) 0.39   (8) 0.625

(9) 0.23   (10) 2.875   (11) 0.475   (12) 0.0875

Instructions: First, convert each decimal to a fraction following the technique described on page 8. Next, convert the decimal to a percent according to the instructions on page 9.

(1) 0.14

(2) 0.1625

(3) 4.75

(4) 7.5

(5) 1.875

(6) 0.4125

(7) 0.2375

(8) 0.12

(9) 0.12

(10) 0.25

(11) 1.35

(12) 0.0675

Instructions: First, convert each decimal to a fraction following the technique described on page 8. Next, convert the decimal to a percent according to the instructions on page 9.

(1) 0.7

(2) 0.0025

(3) 12.5

(4) 1.625

(5) 12.5

(6) 1.5625

(7) 0.29

(8) 1.375

(9) 0.3625

(10) 0.2625

(11) 0.0225

(12) 5.25

Instructions: First, convert each decimal to a fraction following the technique described on page 8. Next, convert the decimal to a percent according to the instructions on page 9.

(1) 0.52   (2) 0.775   (3) 2.5   (4) 0.0325

(5) 0.48   (6) 2.25   (7) 3.9   (8) 2.2

(9) 3.75   (10) 0.925   (11) 0.875   (12) 0.0925

Chapter 3: Converting Percents to Fractions and Decimals

Instructions: First, convert each percent to a decimal following the instructions on page 9. Next, convert the decimal to a fraction according to the technique described on page 8.

(1) 25%   (2) 150%   (3) 80%   (4) 35%

(5) 10%   (6) 12.5%   (7) 375%   (8) 0.5%

(9) 1.5%   (10) 130%   (11) 37.5%   (12) 205%

Instructions: First, convert each percent to a decimal following the instructions on page 9. Next, convert the decimal to a fraction according to the technique described on page 8.

(1) 32.5%   (2) 575%   (3) 450%   (4) 270%

(5) 116%   (6) 460%   (7) 360%   (8) 10%

(9) 390%   (10) 150%   (11) 137.5%   (12) 9.75%

Instructions: First, convert each percent to a decimal following the instructions on page 9. Next, convert the decimal to a fraction according to the technique described on page 8.

(1) 118.75%   (2) 60%   (3) 105%   (4) 106.25%

(5) 6.75%   (6) 5.25%   (7) 45%   (8) 23%

(9) 4.5%   (10) 75%   (11) 210%   (12) 1.75%

Instructions: First, convert each percent to a decimal following the instructions on page 9. Next, convert the decimal to a fraction according to the technique described on page 8.

(1) 6.25%   (2) 87.5%   (3) 270%   (4) 24%

(5) 48%   (6) 195%   (7) 10.5%   (8) 81.25%

(9) 112.5%   (10) 5.75%   (11) 57.5%   (12) 320%

Instructions: First, convert each percent to a decimal following the instructions on page 9. Next, convert the decimal to a fraction according to the technique described on page 8.

(1) 26.25%   (2) 625%   (3) 41.25%   (4) 90%

(5) 18.75%   (6) 180%   (7) 8.75%   (8) 237.5%

(9) 30%   (10) 112.5%   (11) 131.25%   (12) 375%

Instructions: First, convert each percent to a decimal following the instructions on page 9. Next, convert the decimal to a fraction according to the technique described on page 8.

(1) 1050%   (2) 3.75%   (3) 120%   (4) 125%

(5) 165%   (6) 260%   (7) 5.5%   (8) 287.5%

(9) 68%   (10) 60%   (11) 225%   (12) 46.25%

Instructions: First, convert each percent to a decimal following the instructions on page 9. Next, convert the decimal to a fraction according to the technique described on page 8.

(1) 19%   (2) 68%   (3) 7.25%   (4) 2.25%

(5) 96%   (6) 520%   (7) 28.75%   (8) 1250%

(9) 10.5%   (10) 625%   (11) 110%   (12) 16.25%

Instructions: First, convert each percent to a decimal following the instructions on page 9. Next, convert the decimal to a fraction according to the technique described on page 8.

(1) 87.5%   (2) 12.5%   (3) 46%   (4) 140%

(5) 28.75%   (6) 33%   (7) 262.5%   (8) 475%

(9) 19.5%   (10) 2.25%   (11) 237.5%   (12) 312.5%

Instructions: First, convert each percent to a decimal following the instructions on page 9. Next, convert the decimal to a fraction according to the technique described on page 8.

(1) 480%   (2) 4.75%   (3) 35%   (4) 130%

(5) 290%   (6) 38.75%   (7) 115%   (8) 27.5%

(9) 180%   (10) 162.5%   (11) 450%   (12) 50%

Instructions: First, convert each percent to a decimal following the instructions on page 9. Next, convert the decimal to a fraction according to the technique described on page 8.

(1) 290%   (2) 9.25%   (3) 16.25%   (4) 56.25%

(5) 72.5%   (6) 390%   (7) 84%   (8) 130%

(9) 287.5%   (10) 750%   (11) 65%   (12) 17.5%

Instructions: First, convert each percent to a decimal following the instructions on page 9. Next, convert the decimal to a fraction according to the technique described on page 8.

(1) 155%   (2) 260%   (3) 120%   (4) 156.25%

(5) 9.5%   (6) 950%   (7) 6%   (8) 87.5%

(9) 80%   (10) 76%   (11) 1150%   (12) 31.25%

Instructions: First, convert each percent to a decimal following the instructions on page 9. Next, convert the decimal to a fraction according to the technique described on page 8.

(1) 26.25%   (2) 212.5%   (3) 76%   (4) 5.5%

(5) 36%   (6) 237.5%   (7) 325%   (8) 116%

(9) 31.25%   (10) 42.5%   (11) 250%   (12) 131.25%

Instructions: First, convert each percent to a decimal following the instructions on page 9. Next, convert the decimal to a fraction according to the technique described on page 8.

(1) 56.25%   (2) 96%   (3) 237.5%   (4) 350%

(5) 240%   (6) 750%   (7) 0.75%   (8) 6.75%

(9) 62%   (10) 32%   (11) 29%   (12) 96%

Instructions: First, convert each percent to a decimal following the instructions on page 9. Next, convert the decimal to a fraction according to the technique described on page 8.

(1) 87.5%

(2) 475%

(3) 13.75%

(4) 230%

(5) 8%

(6) 43.75%

(7) 112.5%

(8) 210%

(9) 112.5%

(10) 34%

(11) 66%

(12) 156.25%

Instructions: First, convert each percent to a decimal following the instructions on page 9. Next, convert the decimal to a fraction according to the technique described on page 8.

(1) 13.5%   (2) 8.75%   (3) 125%   (4) 48%

(5) 18%   (6) 15.5%   (7) 1050%   (8) 24%

(9) 580%   (10) 15.5%   (11) 650%   (12) 112.5%

Instructions: First, convert each percent to a decimal following the instructions on page 9. Next, convert the decimal to a fraction according to the technique described on page 8.

(1) 2.75%   (2) 95%   (3) 50%   (4) 43.75%

(5) 550%   (6) 143.75%   (7) 75%   (8) 32%

(9) 145%   (10) 8%   (11) 350%   (12) 250%

Instructions: First, convert each percent to a decimal following the instructions on page 9. Next, convert the decimal to a fraction according to the technique described on page 8.

(1) 180%

(2) 82.5%

(3) 8%

(4) 1250%

(5) 150%

(6) 380%

(7) 36%

(8) 237.5%

(9) 250%

(10) 162.5%

(11) 8.75%

(12) 60%

Instructions: First, convert each percent to a decimal following the instructions on page 9. Next, convert the decimal to a fraction according to the technique described on page 8.

(1) 1050%   (2) 9.75%   (3) 48%   (4) 950%

(5) 325%   (6) 1.5%   (7) 180%   (8) 92.5%

(9) 1250%   (10) 118.75%   (11) 475%   (12) 17.5%

Instructions: First, convert each percent to a decimal following the instructions on page 9. Next, convert the decimal to a fraction according to the technique described on page 8.

(1) 15%   (2) 7.5%   (3) 18.5%   (4) 19.5%

(5) 370%   (6) 43.75%   (7) 60%   (8) 118.75%

(9) 4.25%   (10) 32.5%   (11) 212.5%   (12) 22.5%

Instructions: First, convert each percent to a decimal following the instructions on page 9. Next, convert the decimal to a fraction according to the technique described on page 8.

(1) 230%

(2) 165%

(3) 262.5%

(4) 525%

(5) 950%

(6) 145%

(7) 525%

(8) 14.5%

(9) 11.25%

(10) 475%

(11) 46.25%

(12) 350%

Chapter 4: Converting Fractions to Repeating Decimals

Instructions: First, convert each fraction to a decimal following the technique described on page 7. Next, convert the decimal to a percent according to the instructions on page 9.

(1) 2/3   (2) 5/12   (3) 4/11

(4) 7/6   (5) 5/6   (6) 7/36

Instructions: First, convert each fraction to a decimal following the technique described on page 7. Next, convert the decimal to a percent according to the instructions on page 9.

(1) 5/9

(2) 4/15

(3) 7/3

(4) 12/11

(5) 10/27

(6) 1/6

Instructions: First, convert each fraction to a decimal following the technique described on page 7. Next, convert the decimal to a percent according to the instructions on page 9.

(1) 5/18

(2) 10/11

(3) 8/15

(4) 13/30

(5) 9/44

(6) 16/9

Instructions: First, convert each fraction to a decimal following the technique described on page 7. Next, convert the decimal to a percent according to the instructions on page 9.

(1) 8/3

(2) 10/9

(3) 7/36

(4) 4/33

(5) 17/48

(6) 1/12

Instructions: First, convert each fraction to a decimal following the technique described on page 7. Next, convert the decimal to a percent according to the instructions on page 9.

(1) 20/99

(2) 11/30

(3) 17/6

(4) 100/111

(5) 19/66

(6) 11/300

Instructions: First, convert each fraction to a decimal following the technique described on page 7. Next, convert the decimal to a percent according to the instructions on page 9.

(1) 20/3

(2) 19/6

(3) 20/33

(4) 40/11

(5) 100/101

(6) 44/15

Instructions: First, convert each fraction to a decimal following the technique described on page 7. Next, convert the decimal to a percent according to the instructions on page 9.

(1) 13/6   (2) 3/11   (3) 17/12

(4) 24/111   (5) 1/15   (6) 19/36

Instructions: First, convert each fraction to a decimal following the technique described on page 7. Next, convert the decimal to a percent according to the instructions on page 9.

(1) 25/88

(2) 100/27

(3) 16/99

(4) 200/303

(5) 5/18

(6) 7/66

Instructions: First, convert each fraction to a decimal following the technique described on page 7. Next, convert the decimal to a percent according to the instructions on page 9.

(1) 15/88   (2) 8/55   (3) 29/30

(4) 100/27   (5) 20/3   (6) 50/909

Instructions: First, convert each fraction to a decimal following the technique described on page 7. Next, convert the decimal to a percent according to the instructions on page 9.

(1) 16/75

(2) 29/60

(3) 500/111

(4) 1/99

(5) 499/606

(6) 21/22

Instructions: First, convert each fraction to a decimal following the technique described on page 7. Next, convert the decimal to a percent according to the instructions on page 9.

(1) 10/3

(2) 8/33

(3) 199/330

(4) 1000/303

(5) 75/111

(6) 7/6

Instructions: First, convert each fraction to a decimal following the technique described on page 7. Next, convert the decimal to a percent according to the instructions on page 9.

(1) 2/99

(2) 5/12

(3) 4/11

(4) 7/101

(5) 5/44

(6) 101/36

Instructions: First, convert each fraction to a decimal following the technique described on page 7. Next, convert the decimal to a percent according to the instructions on page 9.

(1) 20/9

(2) 25/12

(3) 36/101

(4) 500/1111

(5) 14/27

(6) 199/990

Instructions: First, convert each fraction to a decimal following the technique described on page 7. Next, convert the decimal to a percent according to the instructions on page 9.

(1) 25/144

(2) 55/54

(3) 54/55

(4) 40/9

(5) 50/11

(6) 100/3

Instructions: First, convert each fraction to a decimal following the technique described on page 7. Next, convert the decimal to a percent according to the instructions on page 9.

(1) 19/44

(2) 49/48

(3) 22/15

(4) 14/11

(5) 601/300

(6) 37/88

Instructions: First, convert each fraction to a decimal following the technique described on page 7. Next, convert the decimal to a percent according to the instructions on page 9.

(1) 50/9

(2) 3/7

(3) 101/44

(4) 13/12

(5) 8/15

(6) 19/36

Instructions: First, convert each fraction to a decimal following the technique described on page 7. Next, convert the decimal to a percent according to the instructions on page 9.

(1) 25/33

(2) 7/18

(3) 37/54

(4) 55/48

(5) 29/44

(6) 1000/99

Instructions: First, convert each fraction to a decimal following the technique described on page 7. Next, convert the decimal to a percent according to the instructions on page 9.

(1) 44/27

(2) 41/22

(3) 5/14

(4) 25/144

(5) 98/55

(6) 29/36

Instructions: First, convert each fraction to a decimal following the technique described on page 7. Next, convert the decimal to a percent according to the instructions on page 9.

(1) 25/18   (2) 4/7   (3) 29/12

(4) 1000/909   (5) 23/6   (6) 299/330

Instructions: First, convert each fraction to a decimal following the technique described on page 7. Next, convert the decimal to a percent according to the instructions on page 9.

(1) 64/75

(2) 50/21

(3) 28/33

(4) 35/6

(5) 49/66

(6) 99/111

Chapter 5: Converting Repeating Decimals to Fractions

Instructions: First, convert each decimal to a fraction following the technique described on page 8. Next, convert the decimal to a percent according to the instructions on page 9.

(1) $3.\overline{6}$

(2) $0.\overline{09}$

(3) $0.\overline{8}$

(4) $0.2\overline{3}$

(5) $0.2\overline{6}$

(6) $2.02\overline{27}$

Instructions: First, convert each decimal to a fraction following the technique described on page 8. Next, convert the decimal to a percent according to the instructions on page 9.

(1) $6.8\overline{3}$

(2) $0.\overline{49}$

(3) $0.\overline{48}$

(4) $0.08\overline{3}$

(5) $0.\overline{12}$

(6) $0.4\overline{3}$

Instructions: First, convert each decimal to a fraction following the technique described on page 8. Next, convert the decimal to a percent according to the instructions on page 9.

(1) $0.\overline{90}$

(2) $3.8\overline{3}$

(3) $2.84\overline{09}$

(4) $1.3\overline{8}$

(5) $0.\overline{1386}$

(6) $0.3541\overline{6}$

Instructions: First, convert each decimal to a fraction following the technique described on page 8. Next, convert the decimal to a percent according to the instructions on page 9.

(1) $1.1\overline{3}$

(2) $0.0\overline{51}$

(3) $0.1\overline{96}$

(4) $3.8\overline{6}$

(5) $0.852\overline{27}$

(6) $0.\overline{7425}$

Instructions: First, convert each decimal to a fraction following the technique described on page 8. Next, convert the decimal to a percent according to the instructions on page 9.

(1) $4.\overline{6}$

(2) $0.1736\overline{1}$

(3) $0.38\overline{3}$

(4) $0.8\overline{63}$

(5) $0.3\overline{2838}$

(6) $0.6\overline{3}$

Instructions: First, convert each decimal to a fraction following the technique described on page 8. Next, convert the decimal to a percent according to the instructions on page 9.

(1) $1.\overline{8}$

(2) $0.38\overline{3}$

(3) $5.2\overline{7}$

(4) $0.\overline{21}$

(5) $0.3\overline{2}$

(6) $0.\overline{14}$

Instructions: First, convert each decimal to a fraction following the technique described on page 8. Next, convert the decimal to a percent according to the instructions on page 9.

(1) $0.80\overline{5}$

(2) $0.8\overline{91}$

(3) $0.10\overline{6}$

(4) $1.70\overline{45}$

(5) $0.7\overline{72}$

(6) $4.8\overline{3}$

Instructions: First, convert each decimal to a fraction following the technique described on page 8. Next, convert the decimal to a percent according to the instructions on page 9.

(1) $0.\overline{900}$

(2) $3.\overline{7}$

(3) $0.61\overline{36}$

(4) $0.1\overline{3}$

(5) $0.1\overline{12}$

(6) $0.80\overline{5}$

Instructions: First, convert each decimal to a fraction following the technique described on page 8. Next, convert the decimal to a percent according to the instructions on page 9.

(1) $5.8\overline{3}$　　　　　　(2) $0.7708\overline{3}$　　　　　　(3) $1.0\overline{5}$

(4) $1.\overline{5}$　　　　　　(5) $0.52\overline{27}$　　　　　　(6) $0.\overline{3600}$

Instructions: First, convert each decimal to a fraction following the technique described on page 8. Next, convert the decimal to a percent according to the instructions on page 9.

(1) $1.08\overline{3}$

(2) $0.3\overline{27}$

(3) $0.1\overline{02}$

(4) $0.0\overline{5}$

(5) $1.4\overline{69}$

(6) $0.\overline{0825}$

Instructions: First, convert each decimal to a fraction following the technique described on page 8. Next, convert the decimal to a percent according to the instructions on page 9.

(1) $0.1\overline{36}$

(2) $0.\overline{89}$

(3) $1.33\overline{6}$

(4) $0.43\overline{18}$

(5) $0.\overline{925}$

(6) $3.\overline{78}$

Instructions: First, convert each decimal to a fraction following the technique described on page 8. Next, convert the decimal to a percent according to the instructions on page 9.

(1) $0.2\overline{57}$

(2) $8.\overline{3}$

(3) $0.1\overline{814}$

(4) $1.8\overline{36}$

(5) $1.0\overline{6}$

(6) $0.\overline{4950}$

Instructions: First, convert each decimal to a fraction following the technique described on page 8. Next, convert the decimal to a percent according to the instructions on page 9.

(1) $0.4\overline{629}$

(2) $0.0208\overline{3}$

(3) $0.9\overline{4}$

(4) $0.2\overline{7}$

(5) $0.\overline{1485}$

(6) $0.\overline{8800}$

Instructions: First, convert each decimal to a fraction following the technique described on page 8. Next, convert the decimal to a percent according to the instructions on page 9.

(1) $5.08\overline{3}$

(2) $0.3\overline{06}$

(3) $2.\overline{36}$

(4) $0.\overline{40}$

(5) $0.\overline{3300}$

(6) $0.41\overline{6}$

Instructions: First, convert each decimal to a fraction following the technique described on page 8. Next, convert the decimal to a percent according to the instructions on page 9.

(1) $0.1\overline{4}$

(2) $3.7\overline{72}$

(3) $0.2\overline{6}$

(4) $2.65\overline{3}$

(5) $2.\overline{962}$

(6) $1.\overline{6}$

Instructions: First, convert each decimal to a fraction following the technique described on page 8. Next, convert the decimal to a percent according to the instructions on page 9.

(1) $0.\overline{30}$

(2) $0.11\overline{6}$

(3) $1.1\overline{6}$

(4) $0.0\overline{3}$

(5) $0.9\overline{8}$

(6) $2.\overline{2}$

Instructions: First, convert each decimal to a fraction following the technique described on page 8. Next, convert the decimal to a percent according to the instructions on page 9.

(1) $1.\overline{148}$

(2) $0.91\overline{6}$

(3) $1.11\overline{36}$

(4) $0.\overline{45}$

(5) $0.\overline{4500}$

(6) $1.0208\overline{3}$

Instructions: First, convert each decimal to a fraction following the technique described on page 8. Next, convert the decimal to a percent according to the instructions on page 9.

(1) $16.\overline{6}$

(2) $0.1597\overline{2}$

(3) $0.\overline{1485}$

(4) $0.9\overline{3}$

(5) $0.89\overline{72}$

(6) $0.97\overline{2}$

Instructions: First, convert each decimal to a fraction following the technique described on page 8. Next, convert the decimal to a percent according to the instructions on page 9.

(1) $0.99\overline{6}$

(2) $0.07\overline{755}$

(3) $1.3819\overline{4}$

(4) $1.18\overline{3}$

(5) $2.5\overline{3}$

(6) $0.420\overline{45}$

Instructions: First, convert each decimal to a fraction following the technique described on page 8. Next, convert the decimal to a percent according to the instructions on page 9.

(1) $0.13\overline{8}$

(2) $4.08\overline{3}$

(3) $0.\overline{40}$

(4) $0.2\overline{037}$

(5) $0.\overline{54}$

(6) $1.68\overline{3}$

Answer Key

Chapter 1 Answers:

Page 10
(1) 0.5, 50% (2) 0.7, 70% (3) 0.4, 40% (4) 1.25, 125%
(5) 0.375, 37.5% (6) 0.16, 16% (7) 0.0625, 6.25% (8) 0.35, 35%
(9) 0.2, 20% (10) 2.25, 225% (11) 2.5, 250% (12) 0.14, 14%

Page 11
(1) 0.0025, 0.25% (2) 3.8, 380% (3) 2.375, 237.5% (4) 0.575, 57.5%
(5) 0.24, 24% (6) 0.58, 58% (7) 0.975, 97.5% (8) 2.7, 270%
(9) 0.17, 17% (10) 0.21, 21% (11) 0.32, 32% (12) 2.8, 280%

Page 12
(1) 1.05, 105% (2) 3.5, 350% (3) 0.1625, 16.25% (4) 1.7, 170%
(5) 1.0625, 106.25% (6) 3.125, 312.5% (7) 3.3, 330% (8) 0.2125, 21.25%
(9) 1.85, 185% (10) 3.75, 375% (11) 0.21, 21% (12) 0.08, 8%

Page 13
(1) 4.25, 425% (2) 4.8, 480% (3) 0.11, 11% (4) 0.0625, 6.25%
(5) 0.3625, 36.25% (6) 0.0075, 0.75% (7) 2.75, 275% (8) 1.45, 145%
(9) 0.8125, 81.25% (10) 11.5, 1150% (11) 0.54, 54% (12) 1.5625, 156.25%

Page 14
(1) 0.025, 2.5% (2) 0.17, 17% (3) 1.1875, 118.75% (4) 0.0225, 2.25%
(5) 0.8125, 81.25% (6) 0.85, 85% (7) 2.125, 212.5% (8) 0.045, 4.5%
(9) 0.23, 23% (10) 0.0975, 9.75% (11) 0.375, 37.5% (12) 0.38, 38%

Page 15
(1) 0.75, 75% (2) 0.48, 48% (3) 5.4, 540% (4) 0.27, 27%
(5) 0.11, 11% (6) 1.25, 125% (7) 0.92, 92% (8) 1.375, 137.5%
(9) 9.5, 950% (10) 1.0625, 106.25% (11) 0.2125, 21.25% (12) 1.55, 155%

Page 16
(1) 0.475, 47.5% (2) 2.1, 210% (3) 0.005, 0.5% (4) 0.425, 42.5%
(5) 0.7, 70% (6) 0.54, 54% (7) 0.54, 54% (8) 0.0625, 6.25%
(9) 4.2, 420% (10) 0.92, 92% (11) 0.8, 80% (12) 0.48, 48%

Page 17
(1) 0.155, 15.5% (2) 0.02, 2% (3) 0.74, 74% (4) 0.28, 28%
(5) 0.85, 85% (6) 5.75, 575% (7) 0.115, 11.5% (8) 0.5625, 56.25%
(9) 3.75, 375% (10) 3.4, 340% (11) 0.175, 17.5% (12) 1.95, 195%

Page 18
(1) 8.5, 850% (2) 0.425, 42.5% (3) 0.62, 62% (4) 0.31, 31%
(5) 0.72, 72% (6) 2.1, 210% (7) 2.875, 287.5% (8) 4.25, 425%
(9) 1.375, 137.5% (10) 5.75, 575% (11) 3.1, 310% (12) 0.07, 7%

Page 19
(1) 2.1, 210% (2) 0.0775, 7.75% (3) 0.0425, 4.25% (4) 0.35, 35%
(5) 0.5625, 56.25% (6) 2.3, 230% (7) 6.5, 650% (8) 3.1, 310%
(9) 0.375, 37.5% (10) 2.4, 240% (11) 2.25, 225% (12) 0.42, 42%

Page 20
(1) 0.125, 12.5% (2) 1.16, 116% (3) 0.5625, 56.25% (4) 10.5, 1050%
(5) 0.75, 75% (6) 0.31, 31% (7) 0.045, 4.5% (8) 0.225, 22.5%
(9) 0.425, 42.5% (10) 0.78, 78% (11) 5.6, 560% (12) 1.1, 110%
Page 21
(1) 0.17, 17% (2) 0.7, 70% (3) 1.12, 112% (4) 0.0625, 6.25%
(5) 0.775, 77.5% (6) 0.0225, 2.25% (7) 1.125, 112.5% (8) 0.88, 88%
(9) 0.0325, 3.25% (10) 3.125, 312.5% (11) 1.4375, 143.75% (12) 0.32, 32%
Page 22
(1) 0.1625, 16.25% (2) 0.035, 3.5% (3) 4.25, 425% (4) 0.325, 32.5%
(5) 0.12, 12% (6) 0.08, 8% (7) 0.0525, 5.25% (8) 2.125, 212.5%
(9) 0.74, 74% (10) 0.55, 55% (11) 5.25, 525% (12) 0.3875, 38.75%
Page 23
(1) 0.4625, 46.25% (2) 6.25, 625% (3) 0.0275, 2.75% (4) 0.5625, 56.25%
(5) 0.175, 17.5% (6) 0.825, 82.5% (7) 1.0625, 106.25% (8) 0.1125, 11.25%
(9) 1.08, 108% (10) 0.08, 8% (11) 0.78, 78% (12) 0.2, 20%
Page 24
(1) 0.195, 19.5% (2) 0.105, 10.5% (3) 5.75, 575% (4) 0.26, 26%
(5) 0.16, 16% (6) 0.22, 22% (7) 0.875, 87.5% (8) 0.0725, 7.25%
(9) 0.675, 67.5% (10) 0.9, 90% (11) 5.8, 580% (12) 0.775, 77.5%
Page 25
(1) 0.1875, 18.75% (2) 0.25, 25% (3) 0.03, 3% (4) 1.55, 155%
(5) 0.02, 2% (6) 0.72, 72% (7) 0.0325, 3.25% (8) 0.8125, 81.25%
(9) 1.25, 125% (10) 0.0625, 6.25% (11) 2.125, 212.5% (12) 0.1, 10%
Page 26
(1) 1.3125, 131.25% (2) 0.16, 16% (3) 0.0525, 5.25% (4) 1.3, 130%
(5) 1.625, 162.5% (6) 2.75, 275% (7) 0.24, 24% (8) 0.42, 42%
(9) 1.12, 112% (10) 0.0775, 7.75% (11) 6.5, 650% (12) 1.7, 170%
Page 27
(1) 1.35, 135% (2) 0.115, 11.5% (3) 1.8, 180% (4) 0.135, 13.5%
(5) 0.0725, 7.25% (6) 0.4375, 43.75% (7) 2.375, 237.5% (8) 3.1, 310%
(9) 1.25, 125% (10) 0.975, 97.5% (11) 2.875, 287.5% (12) 0.095, 9.5%
Page 28
(1) 0.4625, 46.25% (2) 2.625, 262.5% (3) 1.5625, 156.25% (4) 0.055, 5.5%
(5) 0.1625, 16.25% (6) 0.9375, 93.75% (7) 5.6, 560% (8) 2.875, 287.5%
(9) 0.06, 6% (10) 0.26, 26% (11) 0.58, 58% (12) 1.1875, 118.75%
Page 29
(1) 0.5, 50% (2) 0.225, 22.5% (3) 1.25, 125% (4) 0.3, 30%
(5) 0.36, 36% (6) 1.5625, 156.25% (7) 0.14, 14% (8) 0.62, 62%
(9) 0.29, 29% (10) 0.2375, 23.75% (11) 1.85, 185% (12) 0.31, 31%

Chapter 2 Answers:

Page 30
(1) 3/4, 75% (2) 1/10, 10% (3) 5/2, 250% (4) 3/10, 30%
(5) 16/5, 320% (6) 3/8, 37.5% (7) 5/4, 125% (8) 4/5, 80%
(9) 1/2, 50% (10) 1/100, 1% (11) 1/20, 5% (12) 19/20, 95%
Page 31
(1) 7/16, 43.75%(2) 15/4, 375%(3) 17/400, 4.25%(4) 3/2, 150%
(5) 25/16, 156.25%(6) 33/400, 8.25%(7) 21/25, 84%(8) 39/50, 78%
(9) 19/400, 4.75%(10) 1/20, 5%(11) 1/5, 20%(12) 28/25, 112%
Page 32
(1) 25/4, 625%(2) 9/200, 4.5%(3) 29/10, 290%(4) 7/2, 350%
(5) 29/10, 290%(6) 11/16, 68.75%(7) 7/2, 350%(8) 13/50, 26%
(9) 5/8, 62.5%(10) 9/40, 22.5%(11) 19/2, 950%(12) 3/10, 30%
Page 33
(1) 21/8, 262.5%(2) 19/400, 4.75%(3) 1/4, 25%(4) 9/20, 45%
(5) 4/25, 16%(6) 13/400, 3.25%(7) 7/10, 70%(8) 5/2, 250%
(9) 7/50, 14%(10) 1/4, 25%(11) 9/8, 112.5%(12) 13/8, 162.5%
Page 34
(1) 29/100, 29%(2) 23/10, 230%(3) 27/400, 6.75%(4) 21/400, 5.25%
(5) 1/16, 6.25%(6) 27/80, 33.75%(7) 23/80, 28.75%(8) 33/80, 41.25%
(9) 16/25, 64%(10) 13/2, 650%(11) 5/4, 125%(12) 15/4, 375%
Page 35
(1) 7/100, 7%(2) 15/2, 750%(3) 1/200, 0.5%(4) 17/5, 340%
(5) 21/50, 42%(6) 7/2, 350%(7) 7/100, 7%(8) 19/10, 190%
(9) 11/40, 27.5%(10) 27/20, 135%(11) 21/50, 42%(12) 1/50, 2%
Page 36
(1) 12/25, 48%(2) 7/16, 43.75%(3) 7/100, 7%(4) 17/20, 85%
(5) 21/20, 105%(6) 7/40, 17.5%(7) 5/4, 125%(8) 29/20, 145%
(9) 3/100, 3%(10) 21/10, 210%(11) 23/100, 23%(12) 29/50, 58%
Page 37
(1) 13/200, 6.5%(2) 13/5, 260%(3) 18/5, 360%(4) 21/16, 131.25%
(5) 39/400, 9.75%(6) 11/100, 11%(7) 19/2, 950%(8) 11/4, 275%
(9) 19/16, 118.75%(10) 15/2, 750%(11) 13/8, 162.5%(12) 33/400, 8.25%
Page 38
(1) 11/8, 137.5%(2) 1/400, 0.25%(3) 17/50, 34%(4) 7/16, 43.75%
(5) 4/5, 80%(6) 1/50, 2%(7) 15/8, 187.5%(8) 2/25, 8%
(9) 23/2, 1150%(10) 9/40, 22.5%(11) 29/10, 290%(12) 5/2, 250%
Page 39
(1) 33/40, 82.5%(2) 13/2, 650%(3) 3/20, 15%(4) 9/2, 450%
(5) 23/8, 287.5%(6) 2/5, 40%(7) 21/2, 1050%(8) 22/25, 88%
(9) 33/50, 66%(10) 19/8, 237.5%(11) 33/40, 82.5%(12) 33/10, 330%

Page 40

(1) 13/40, 32.5%(2) 23/50, 46%(3) 11/10, 110%(4) 37/20, 185%

(5) 17/16, 106.25%(6) 21/8, 262.5%(7) 19/8, 237.5%(8) 13/25, 52%

(9) 7/20, 35%(10) 21/40, 52.5%(11) 39/40, 97.5%(12) 21/4, 525%

Page 41

(1) 3/200, 1.5%(2) 1/8, 12.5%(3) 25/8, 312.5%(4) 5/2, 250%

(5) 7/80, 8.75%(6) 17/50, 34%(7) 25/16, 156.25%(8) 7/400, 1.75%

(9) 17/8, 212.5%(10) 13/4, 325%(11) 11/40, 27.5%(12) 33/100, 33%

Page 42

(1) 1/8, 12.5%(2) 29/50, 58%(3) 9/20, 45%(4) 19/40, 47.5%

(5) 19/100, 19%(6) 5/4, 125%(7) 11/4, 275%(8) 7/5, 140%

(9) 19/40, 47.5%(10) 11/40, 27.5%(11) 25/8, 312.5%(12) 1/100, 1%

Page 43

(1) 13/50, 26%(2) 23/50, 46%(3) 39/40, 97.5%(4) 23/16, 143.75%

(5) 6/25, 24%(6) 25/8, 312.5%(7) 17/40, 42.5%(8) 9/8, 112.5%

(9) 9/4, 225%(10) 39/40, 97.5%(11) 24/25, 96%(12) 1/16, 6.25%

Page 44

(1) 33/50, 66%(2) 25/8, 312.5%(3) 21/8, 262.5%(4) 11/16, 68.75%

(5) 25/8, 312.5%(6) 17/20, 85%(7) 17/25, 68%(8) 9/5, 180%

(9) 27/400, 6.75%(10) 21/10, 210%(11) 19/16, 118.75%(12) 3/400, 0.75%

Page 45

(1) 23/8, 287.5%(2) 3/25, 12%(3) 7/5, 140%(4) 9/2, 450%

(5) 7/25, 28%(6) 3/20, 15%(7) 7/80, 8.75%(8) 17/4, 425%

(9) 23/16, 143.75%(10) 19/2, 950%(11) 2/25, 8%(12) 21/40, 52.5%

Page 46

(1) 25/4, 625%(2) 23/16, 143.75%(3) 27/10, 270%(4) 11/8, 137.5%

(5) 37/20, 185%(6) 9/5, 180%(7) 39/100, 39%(8) 5/8, 62.5%

(9) 23/100, 23%(10) 23/8, 287.5%(11) 19/40, 47.5%(12) 7/80, 8.75%

Page 47

(1) 7/50, 14%(2) 13/80, 16.25%(3) 19/4, 475%(4) 15/2, 750%

(5) 15/8, 187.5%(6) 33/80, 41.25%(7) 19/80, 23.75%(8) 3/25, 12%

(9) 3/25, 12%(10) 1/4, 25%(11) 27/20, 135%(12) 27/400, 6.75%

Page 48

(1) 7/10, 70%(2) 1/400, 0.25%(3) 25/2, 1250%(4) 13/8, 162.5%

(5) 25/2, 1250%(6) 25/16, 156.25%(7) 29/100, 29%(8) 11/8, 137.5%

(9) 29/80, 36.25%(10) 21/80, 26.25%(11) 9/400, 2.25%(12) 21/4, 525%

Page 49

(1) 13/25, 52%(2) 31/40, 77.5%(3) 5/2, 250%(4) 13/400, 3.25%

(5) 12/25, 48%(6) 9/4, 225%(7) 39/10, 390%(8) 11/5, 220%

(9) 15/4, 375%(10) 37/40, 92.5%(11) 7/8, 87.5%(12) 37/400, 9.25%

Chapter 3 Answers:

Page 50
(1) 1/4, 0.25 (2) 3/2, 1.5 (3) 4/5, 0.8 (4) 7/20, 0.35
(5) 1/10, 0.1 (6) 1/8, 0.125 (7) 15/4, 3.75 (8) 1/200, 0.005
(9) 3/200, 0.015 (10) 13/10, 1.3 (11) 3/8, 0.375 (12) 41/20, 2.05
Page 51
(1) 13/40, 0.325(2) 23/4, 5.75(3) 9/2, 4.5(4) 27/10, 2.7
(5) 29/25, 1.16(6) 23/5, 4.6(7) 18/5, 3.6(8) 1/10, 0.1
(9) 39/10, 3.9(10) 3/2, 1.5(11) 11/8, 1.375(12) 39/400, 0.0975
Page 52
(1) 19/16, 1.1875(2) 3/5, 0.6(3) 21/20, 1.05(4) 17/16, 1.0625
(5) 27/400, 0.0675(6) 21/400, 0.0525(7) 9/20, 0.45(8) 23/100, 0.23
(9) 9/200, 0.045(10) 3/4, 0.75(11) 21/10, 2.1(12) 7/400, 0.0175
Page 53
(1) 1/16, 0.0625(2) 7/8, 0.875(3) 27/10, 2.7(4) 6/25, 0.24
(5) 12/25, 0.48(6) 39/20, 1.95(7) 21/200, 0.105(8) 13/16, 0.8125
(9) 9/8, 1.125(10) 23/400, 0.0575(11) 23/40, 0.575(12) 16/5, 3.2
Page 54
(1) 21/80, 0.2625(2) 25/4, 6.25(3) 33/80, 0.4125(4) 9/10, 0.9
(5) 3/16, 0.1875(6) 9/5, 1.8(7) 7/80, 0.0875(8) 19/8, 2.375
(9) 3/10, 0.3(10) 9/8, 1.125(11) 21/16, 1.3125(12) 15/4, 3.75
Page 55
(1) 21/2, 10.5(2) 3/80, 0.0375(3) 6/5, 1.2(4) 5/4, 1.25
(5) 33/20, 1.65(6) 13/5, 2.6(7) 11/200, 0.055(8) 23/8, 2.875
(9) 17/25, 0.68(10) 3/5, 0.6(11) 9/4, 2.25(12) 37/80, 0.4625
Page 56
(1) 19/100, 0.19(2) 17/25, 0.68(3) 29/400, 0.0725(4) 9/400, 0.0225
(5) 24/25, 0.96(6) 26/5, 5.2(7) 23/80, 0.2875(8) 25/2, 12.5
(9) 21/200, 0.105(10) 25/4, 6.25(11) 11/10, 1.1(12) 13/80, 0.1625
Page 57
(1) 7/8, 0.875(2) 1/8, 0.125(3) 23/50, 0.46(4) 7/5, 1.4
(5) 23/80, 0.2875(6) 33/100, 0.33(7) 21/8, 2.625(8) 19/4, 4.75
(9) 39/200, 0.195(10) 9/400, 0.0225(11) 19/8, 2.375(12) 25/8, 3.125
Page 58
(1) 24/5, 4.8(2) 19/400, 0.0475(3) 7/20, 0.35(4) 13/10, 1.3
(5) 29/10, 2.9(6) 31/80, 0.3875(7) 23/20, 1.15(8) 11/40, 0.275
(9) 9/5, 1.8(10) 13/8, 1.625(11) 9/2, 4.5(12) 1/2, 0.5
Page 59
(1) 29/10, 2.9(2) 37/400, 0.0925(3) 13/80, 0.1625(4) 9/16, 0.5625
(5) 29/40, 0.725(6) 39/10, 3.9(7) 21/25, 0.84(8) 13/10, 1.3
(9) 23/8, 2.875(10) 15/2, 7.5(11) 13/20, 0.65(12) 7/40, 0.175

Page 60

(1) 31/20, 1.55(2) 13/5, 2.6(3) 6/5, 1.2(4) 25/16, 1.5625

(5) 19/200, 0.095(6) 19/2, 9.5(7) 3/50, 0.06(8) 7/8, 0.875

(9) 4/5, 0.8(10) 19/25, 0.76(11) 23/2, 11.5(12) 5/16, 0.3125

Page 61

(1) 21/80, 0.2625(2) 17/8, 2.125(3) 19/25, 0.76(4) 11/200, 0.055

(5) 9/25, 0.36(6) 19/8, 2.375(7) 13/4, 3.25(8) 29/25, 1.16

(9) 5/16, 0.3125(10) 17/40, 0.425(11) 5/2, 2.5(12) 21/16, 1.3125

Page 62

(1) 9/16, 0.5625(2) 24/25, 0.96(3) 19/8, 2.375(4) 7/2, 3.5

(5) 12/5, 2.4(6) 15/2, 7.5(7) 3/400, 0.0075(8) 27/400, 0.0675

(9) 31/50, 0.62(10) 8/25, 0.32(11) 29/100, 0.29(12) 24/25, 0.96

Page 63

(1) 7/8, 0.875(2) 19/4, 4.75(3) 11/80, 0.1375(4) 23/10, 2.3

(5) 2/25, 0.08(6) 7/16, 0.4375(7) 9/8, 1.125(8) 21/10, 2.1

(9) 9/8, 1.125(10) 17/50, 0.34(11) 33/50, 0.66(12) 25/16, 1.5625

Page 64

(1) 27/200, 0.135(2) 7/80, 0.0875(3) 5/4, 1.25(4) 12/25, 0.48

(5) 9/50, 0.18(6) 31/200, 0.155(7) 21/2, 10.5(8) 6/25, 0.24

(9) 29/5, 5.8(10) 31/200, 0.155(11) 13/2, 6.5(12) 9/8, 1.125

Page 65

(1) 11/400, 0.0275(2) 19/20, 0.95(3) 1/2, 0.5(4) 7/16, 0.4375

(5) 11/2, 5.5(6) 23/16, 1.4375(7) 3/4, 0.75(8) 8/25, 0.32

(9) 29/20, 1.45(10) 2/25, 0.08(11) 7/2, 3.5(12) 5/2, 2.5

Page 66

(1) 9/5, 1.8(2) 33/40, 0.825(3) 2/25, 0.08(4) 25/2, 12.5

(5) 3/2, 1.5(6) 19/5, 3.8(7) 9/25, 0.36(8) 19/8, 2.375

(9) 5/2, 2.5(10) 13/8, 1.625(11) 7/80, 0.0875(12) 3/5, 0.6

Page 67

(1) 21/2, 10.5(2) 39/400, 0.0975(3) 12/25, 0.48(4) 19/2, 9.5

(5) 13/4, 3.25(6) 3/200, 0.015(7) 9/5, 1.8(8) 37/40, 0.925

(9) 25/2, 12.5(10) 19/16, 1.1875(11) 19/4, 4.75(12) 7/40, 0.175

Page 68

(1) 3/20, 0.15(2) 3/40, 0.075(3) 37/200, 0.185(4) 39/200, 0.195

(5) 37/10, 3.7(6) 7/16, 0.4375(7) 3/5, 0.6(8) 19/16, 1.1875

(9) 17/400, 0.0425(10) 13/40, 0.325(11) 17/8, 2.125(12) 9/40, 0.225

Page 69

(1) 23/10, 2.3(2) 33/20, 1.65(3) 21/8, 2.625(4) 21/4, 5.25

(5) 19/2, 9.5(6) 29/20, 1.45(7) 21/4, 5.25(8) 29/200, 0.145

(9) 9/80, 0.1125(10) 19/4, 4.75(11) 37/80, 0.4625(12) 7/2, 3.5

Chapter 4 Answers:

Page 70
(1) $0.\overline{6}$, $66.\overline{6}\%$ (2) $0.41\overline{6}$, $41.\overline{6}\%$ (3) $0.\overline{36}$, $36.\overline{36}\%$
(4) $1.1\overline{6}$, $116.\overline{6}\%$ (5) $0.8\overline{3}$, $83.\overline{3}\%$ (6) $0.19\overline{4}$, $19.\overline{4}\%$

Page 71
(1) $0.\overline{5}$, $55.\overline{5}\%$ (2) $0.2\overline{6}$, $26.\overline{6}\%$ (3) $2.\overline{3}$, $233.\overline{3}\%$
(4) $1.\overline{09}$, $109.\overline{09}\%$ (5) $0.\overline{370}$, $37.\overline{037}\%$ (6) $0.1\overline{6}$, $16.\overline{6}\%$

Page 72
(1) $0.2\overline{7}$, $27..\overline{7}\%$ (2) $0.\overline{09}$, $90.\overline{90}\%$ (3) $0.5\overline{37}$, $53.\overline{3}\%$
(4) $0.4\overline{3}$, $43.\overline{3}\%$ (5) $0.20\overline{45}$, $20.\overline{45}\%$ (6) $1.\overline{7}$, $177.\overline{7}\%$

Page 73
(1) $2.\overline{6}$, $266.\overline{6}\%$ (2) $1.\overline{1}$, $111.\overline{1}\%$ (3) $0.19\overline{4}$, $19.\overline{4}\%$
(4) $0.\overline{12}$, $12.\overline{12}\%$ (5) $0.3541\overline{6}$, $35.41\overline{6}\%$ (6) $0.08\overline{3}$, $8.\overline{3}\%$

Page 74
(1) $0.\overline{20}$, $20.\overline{20}\%$ (2) $0.3\overline{6}$, $36.\overline{6}\%$ (3) $2.8\overline{3}$, $283.\overline{3}\%$
(4) $0.\overline{900}$, $90.\overline{090}\%$ (5) $0.28\overline{7}$, $28.7\overline{8}\%$ (6) $0.03\overline{6}$, $3.\overline{6}\%$

Page 75
(1) $6.\overline{6}$, $666.\overline{6}\%$ (2) $3.1\overline{6}$, $316.\overline{6}\%$ (3) $0.\overline{60}$, $60.\overline{60}\%$
(4) $3.\overline{63}$, $363.\overline{63}\%$ (5) $0.\overline{9900}$, $99.\overline{0099}\%$ (6) $2.9\overline{3}$, $293.\overline{3}\%$

Page 76
(1) $2.1\overline{6}$, $216.\overline{6}\%$ (2) $0.\overline{27}$, $27.\overline{27}\%$ (3) $1.41\overline{6}$, $141.\overline{6}\%$
(4) $0.\overline{216}$, $21.\overline{621}\%$ (5) $0.0\overline{6}$, $6.\overline{6}\%$ (6) $0.52\overline{7}$, 52.7%

Page 77
(1) $0.284\overline{09}$, $28.4\overline{09}\%$ (2) $3.\overline{703}$, $370.\overline{370}\%$ (3) $0.\overline{16}$, $16.\overline{16}\%$
(4) $0.\overline{6600}$, $66.\overline{0066}\%$ (5) $0.2\overline{7}$, $27.\overline{7}\%$ (6) $0.10\overline{6}$, $10.\overline{60}\%$

Page 78
(1) $0.170\overline{45}$, $17.0\overline{45}\%$ (2) $0.1\overline{45}$, $14.\overline{54}\%$ (3) $0.9\overline{6}$, $96.\overline{6}\%$
(4) $3.\overline{703}$, $370.\overline{370}\%$ (5) $6.\overline{6}$, $666.\overline{6}\%$ (6) $0.\overline{0550}$, $5.\overline{5005}\%$

Page 79
(1) $0.21\overline{3}$, $21.\overline{3}\%$ (2) $0.48\overline{3}$, $48.\overline{3}\%$ (3) $4.\overline{504}$, $450.\overline{450}\%$
(4) $0.\overline{01}$, $1.\overline{01}\%$ (5) $0.82\overline{343}$, $82.\overline{3432}\%$ (6) $0.9\overline{54}$, $95.\overline{45}\%$

Page 80
(1) $3.\overline{3}$, $333.\overline{3}\%$ (2) $0.\overline{24}$, $24.\overline{24}\%$ (3) $0.60\overline{3}$, $60.\overline{30}\%$
(4) $3.\overline{3003}$, $330.\overline{0330}\%$ (5) $0.67\overline{5}$, $67.\overline{567}\%$ (6) $1.1\overline{6}$, $116.\overline{6}\%$

Page 81
(1) $0.\overline{02}$, $2.\overline{02}\%$ (2) $0.41\overline{6}$, $41.\overline{6}\%$ (3) $0.\overline{36}$, $36.\overline{36}\%$
(4) $0.\overline{0693}$, $6.\overline{9306}\%$ (5) $0.11\overline{36}$, $11.\overline{36}\%$ (6) $2.80\overline{5}$, $280.\overline{5}\%$

Page 82
(1) $2.\overline{2}$, $222.\overline{2}\%$ (2) $2.08\overline{3}$, $208.\overline{3}\%$ (3) $0.\overline{3564}$, $35.\overline{6435}\%$
(4) $0.\overline{4500}$, $45.\overline{0045}\%$ (5) $0.5\overline{18}$, $51.\overline{851}\%$ (6) $0.2\overline{01}$, $20.\overline{10}\%$

Page 83
(1) $0.1736\overline{1}$, $17.36\overline{1}\%$ (2) $1.0\overline{185}$, $101.8\overline{51}\%$ (3) $0.9\overline{81}$, $98.\overline{18}\%$
(4) $4.\overline{4}$, $444.\overline{4}\%$ (5) $4.\overline{54}$, $454.\overline{54}\%$ (6) $33.\overline{3}$, $3333.\overline{3}\%$

Page 84
(1) $0.43\overline{18}$, $43.\overline{18}\%$ (2) $1.0208\overline{3}$, $102.08\overline{3}\%$ (3) $1.4\overline{6}$, $146.\overline{6}\%$
(4) $1.\overline{27}$, $127.\overline{27}\%$ (5) $2.00\overline{3}$, $200.\overline{3}\%$ (6) $0.420\overline{45}$, $42.0\overline{45}\%$

Page 85
(1) $5.\overline{5}$, $555.\overline{5}\%$ (2) $0.\overline{428571}$, $42.\overline{857142}\%$ (3) $2.29\overline{54}$, $229.\overline{54}\%$
(4) $1.08\overline{3}$, $108.\overline{3}\%$ (5) $0.5\overline{3}$, $53.\overline{3}\%$ (6) $0.52\overline{7}$, $52.\overline{7}\%$

Page 86
(1) $0.\overline{75}$, $75.\overline{75}\%$ (2) $0.3\overline{8}$, $38.\overline{8}\%$ (3) $0.6\overline{851}$, $68.\overline{518}\%$
(4) $1.1458\overline{3}$, $114.58\overline{3}\%$ (5) $0.65\overline{90}$, $65.\overline{90}\%$ (6) $10.\overline{10}$, $1010.\overline{10}\%$

Page 87
(1) $1.\overline{629}$, $162.\overline{962}\%$ (2) $1.8\overline{63}$, $186.\overline{36}\%$ (3) $0.3\overline{571428}$, $35.\overline{714285}\%$
(4) $0.1736\overline{1}$, $17.36\overline{1}\%$ (5) $1.7\overline{81}$, $178.\overline{18}\%$ (6) $0.80\overline{5}$, $80.\overline{5}\%$

Page 88
(1) $1.3\overline{8}$, $138.\overline{8}\%$ (2) $0.\overline{571428}$, $57.\overline{142857}\%$ (3) $2.41\overline{6}$, $241.\overline{6}\%$
(4) $1.\overline{1001}$, $110.0\overline{110}\%$ (5) $3.8\overline{3}$, $383.\overline{3}\%$ (6) $0.9\overline{06}$, $90.\overline{60}\%$

Page 89
(1) $0.85\overline{3}$, $85.\overline{3}\%$ (2) $2.\overline{380952}$, $238.\overline{095238}\%$ (3) $0.\overline{84}$, $84.\overline{84}\%$
(4) $5.8\overline{3}$, $583.\overline{3}\%$ (5) $0.7\overline{42}$, $74.\overline{24}\%$ (6) $0.8\overline{91}$, $89.\overline{189}\%$

Chapter 5 Answers:

Page 90
(1) 11/3, $366.\overline{6}\%$ (2) 1/11, $9.\overline{09}\%$ (3) 8/9, $88.\overline{8}\%$
(4) 7/30, $23.\overline{3}\%$ (5) 4/15, $26.\overline{6}\%$ (6) 89/44, $202.\overline{27}\%$

Page 91
(1) 41/6, $683.\overline{3}\%$ (2) 49/99, $49.\overline{49}\%$ (3) 16/33, $48.\overline{48}\%$
(4) 1/12, $8.\overline{3}\%$ (5) 4/33, $12.\overline{12}\%$ (6) 13/30, $43.\overline{3}\%$

Page 92
(1) 10/11, $90.\overline{90}\%$ (2) 23/6, $383.\overline{3}\%$ (3) 125/44, $284.\overline{09}\%$
(4) 25/18, $138.\overline{8}\%$ (5) 14/101, $13.\overline{8613}\%$ (6) 17/48, $35.41\overline{6}\%$

Page 93
(1) 17/15, $113.\overline{3}\%$ (2) 17/330, $5.1\overline{5}\%$ (3) 13/66, $19.\overline{69}\%$
(4) 23/6, $383.\overline{3}\%$ (5) 75/88, $85.2\overline{27}\%$ (6) 75/101, $74.\overline{2574}\%$

Page 94
(1) 14/3, $466.\overline{6}\%$ (2) 25/144, $17.36\overline{1}\%$ (3) 23/60, $38.\overline{3}\%$
(4) 19/22, $86.\overline{36}\%$ (5) 199/606, $32.8\overline{382}\%$ (6) 57/90, $63.\overline{3}\%$

Page 95
(1) 17/9, 188.$\overline{8}$% (2) 23/60, 38.$\overline{3}$% (3) 95/18, 527.$\overline{7}$%
(4) 7/33, 21.$\overline{21}$% (5) 29/90, 32.$\overline{2}$% (6) 14/99, 14.$\overline{14}$%
Page 96
(1) 29/36, 80.$\overline{5}$% (2) 99/111, 89.$\overline{189}$% (3) 8/75, 10.$\overline{6}$%
(4) 75/44, 170.4$\overline{5}$% (5) 17/22, 77.$\overline{27}$% (6) 29/6, 483.$\overline{3}$%
Page 97
(1) 100/111, 90.$\overline{090}$% (2) 34/9, 377.$\overline{7}$% (3) 27/44, 61.$\overline{36}$%
(4) 2/15, 13.$\overline{3}$% (5) 111/990, 11.$\overline{21}$% (6) 29/36, 80.$\overline{5}$%
Page 98
(1) 35/6, 583.$\overline{3}$% (2) 37/48, 77.08$\overline{3}$% (3) 19/18, 105.$\overline{5}$%
(4) 14/9, 155.$\overline{5}$% (5) 23/44, 52.$\overline{27}$% (6) 400/1111, 36.$\overline{0036}$%
Page 99
(1) 13/12, 108.$\overline{3}$% (2) 18/55, 32.$\overline{72}$% (3) 101/990, 10.$\overline{20}$%
(4) 1/18, 5.$\overline{5}$% (5) 97/66, 146.$\overline{96}$% (6) 25/303, 8.$\overline{2508}$%
Page 100
(1) 3/22, 13.$\overline{63}$% (2) 89/99, 89.$\overline{89}$% (3) 401/300, 133.$\overline{6}$%
(4) 19/44, 43.$\overline{18}$% (5) 25/27, 92.$\overline{592}$% (6) 125/33, 378.$\overline{78}$%
Page 101
(1) 17/66, 25.$\overline{75}$% (2) 25/3, 833.$\overline{3}$% (3) 49/270, 18.$\overline{148}$%
(4) 101/55, 183.$\overline{63}$% (5) 16/15, 106.$\overline{6}$% (6) 50/101, 49.$\overline{5049}$%
Page 102
(1) 25/54, 46.$\overline{296}$% (2) 1/48, 2.08$\overline{3}$% (3) 17/18, 94.$\overline{4}$%
(4) 5/18, 27.$\overline{7}$% (5) 15/101, 14.$\overline{8514}$% (6) 800/909, 88.$\overline{0088}$%
Page 103
(1) 61/12, 508.$\overline{3}$% (2) 101/330, 30.$\overline{60}$% (3) 26/11, 236.$\overline{36}$%
(4) 40/99, 40.$\overline{40}$% (5) 100/303, 33.$\overline{0033}$% (6) 5/12, 41.$\overline{6}$%
Page 104
(1) 13/90, 14.$\overline{4}$% (2) 83/22, 377.$\overline{27}$% (3) 4/15, 26.$\overline{6}$%
(4) 199/75, 265.$\overline{3}$% (5) 80/27, 296.$\overline{296}$% (6) 5/3, 166.$\overline{6}$%
Page 105
(1) 10/33, 30.$\overline{30}$% (2) 7/60, 11.$\overline{6}$% (3) 7/6, 116.$\overline{6}$%
(4) 1/30, 3.$\overline{3}$% (5) 89/90, 98.$\overline{8}$% (6) 20/9, 222.$\overline{2}$%
Page 106
(1) 31/27, 114.$\overline{814}$% (2) 11/12, 91.$\overline{6}$% (3) 49/44, 111.$\overline{36}$%
(4) 5/11, 45.$\overline{45}$% (5) 500/1111, 45.$\overline{0045}$% (6) 49/48, 102.08$\overline{3}$%
Page 107
(1) 50/3, 1666.$\overline{6}$% (2) 23/144, 15.97$\overline{2}$% (3) 15/101, 14.$\overline{8514}$%
(4) 14/15, 93.$\overline{3}$% (5) 79/88, 89.7$\overline{72}$% (6) 35/36, 97.$\overline{2}$%

Page 108
(1) 299/300, 99.$\overline{6}$% (2) 47/606, 7.7$\overline{557}$% (3) 199/144, 138.19$\overline{4}$%
(4) 71/60, 118.$\overline{3}$% (5) 38/15, 253.$\overline{3}$% (6) 37/88, 42.0$\overline{45}$%
Page 109
(1) 5/36, 13.$\overline{8}$% (2) 49/12, 408.$\overline{3}$% (3) 40/99, 40.$\overline{40}$%
(4) 11/54, 20.$\overline{370}$% (5) 6/11, 54.$\overline{54}$% (6) 101/60, 168.$\overline{3}$%

Made in United States
North Haven, CT
26 October 2023

43230524R00067